INSIDE THE
NFL

CAROLINA
PANTHERS

BY TODD RYAN

SportsZone

An Imprint of Abdo Publishing
abdobooks.com

abdobooks.com

Published by Abdo Publishing, a division of ABDO, PO Box 398166, Minneapolis, Minnesota 55439. Copyright © 2020 by Abdo Consulting Group, Inc. International copyrights reserved in all countries. No part of this book may be reproduced in any form without written permission from the publisher. SportsZone™ is a trademark and logo of Abdo Publishing.

Printed in the United States of America, North Mankato, Minnesota
042019
092019

Cover Photo: Tom DiPace/AP Images
Interior Photos: Dave Martin/AP Images, 4–5, 43; Mark J. Terrill/AP Images, 7; Amy Sancetta/AP Images, 9; Chuck Burton/AP Images, 11, 15, 17, 29; Alan Marler/AP Images, 13; Nell Redmond/AP Images, 18; Rusty Burroughs/AP Images, 21; Charles Rex Arbogast/AP Images, 22–23; Chris Gardner/AP Images, 25; Bill Kostroun/AP Images, 26; Rick Havner/AP Images, 31, 33; Stephen Chernin/AP Images, 35; Bob Leverone/AP Images, 37; Julio Cortez/AP Images, 39; Margaret Bowles/AP Images, 41

Editor: Patrick Donnelly
Series Designer: Craig Hinton

Library of Congress Control Number: 2018965351

Publisher's Cataloging-in-Publication Data

Names: Ryan, Todd, author.
Title: Carolina Panthers / by Todd Ryan
Description: Minneapolis, Minnesota: Abdo Publishing, 2020 | Series: Inside the NFL | Includes online resources and index.
Identifiers: ISBN 9781532118401 (lib. bdg.) | ISBN 9781532172588 (ebook) | ISBN 9781644941027 (pbk.)
Subjects: LCSH: Carolina Panthers (Football team)--Juvenile literature. | National Football League--Juvenile literature. | Football teams--Juvenile literature. | American football--Juvenile literature.
Classification: DDC 796.33264--dc23

TABLE OF
CONTENTS

CHAPTER 1

IMPROBABLE RUN

The Carolina Panthers finished 1–15 in 2001. It was the worst record in the National Football League (NFL). Only two seasons later, though, the Panthers were in the Super Bowl for the first time.

But winning the Super Bowl would not be easy. The Panthers were matched up against quarterback Tom Brady and the New England Patriots in Super Bowl XXXVIII. The Patriots were seven-point favorites on February 1, 2004, at Reliant Stadium in Houston.

However, the Panthers believed they could win. And their play on the field showed they were right, as they gave the Patriots all they could handle.

Quarterback Jake Delhomme celebrates after Carolina defeated Philadelphia 14–3 in the NFC Championship Game.

JAKE DELHOMME

Quarterback Jake Delhomme began his NFL career as an undrafted free agent with the New Orleans Saints in 1997. He spent a season on their practice squad. New Orleans then assigned him to the NFL Europe league to gain experience. He helped the Frankfurt Galaxy win World Bowl VII in June 1999.

The Saints brought Delhomme back as a backup quarterback. He saw little playing time through 2002. The Panthers thought he had potential, however, and signed Delhomme as a free agent to back up veteran Rodney Peete.

With Carolina trailing the Jacksonville Jaguars 17–0 in the 2003 opener, head coach John Fox put Delhomme in the game. He went on to throw three touchdown passes, and Carolina won 24–23. Delhomme started the rest of the season. The Panthers went 11–5, won the National Football Conference (NFC) South Division, and made a magical playoff run.

The game was scoreless until late in the second quarter. Then Brady threw a short touchdown pass. The Panthers tied it, but Brady threw another to retake the lead. Finally, as time expired in the first half, Carolina's John Kasay made a 50-yard field goal to cut New England's lead to 14–10.

Neither team scored in the third quarter. But then came one of the most thrilling finishes in Super Bowl history. The Patriots

✗ Carolina's DeShaun Foster dives past New England safety Rodney Harrison to complete a 33-yard touchdown run in Super Bowl XXXVIII.

scored first, putting them up 21–10. But the Panthers clawed back with three big plays to take the lead.

First, running back DeShaun Foster scored on a 33-yard run. When the Patriots threatened to score again, cornerback Reggie Howard intercepted a pass in the end zone. Stuck deep in its own territory, Carolina needed a third big play to tilt the game in its favor. On third down, the Panthers got it. Panthers quarterback Jake Delhomme found wide receiver Muhsin Muhammad for an 85-yard touchdown pass. It set a Super Bowl

POSTSEASON PATH

Carolina's playoff road to the Super Bowl after the 2003 season was not easy. The Panthers beat the visiting Dallas Cowboys 29–10 in the wild-card round. But then things got much trickier. Next up was a road game against the St. Louis Rams. Jake Delhomme's 69-yard touchdown pass to Steve Smith gave the Panthers a thrilling 29–23 win in double overtime. The Panthers then traveled to Philadelphia for the NFC Championship Game. The Eagles had defeated the Panthers 25–16 in Charlotte, North Carolina, late in the regular season. Carolina would not be denied this time, though. Stephen Davis and DeShaun Foster combined for 136 rushing yards. The Panthers won 14–3 to clinch their first Super Bowl appearance.

record for the longest play from scrimmage. After a failed two-point conversion, Carolina led 22–21.

The lead did not last long. Brady drove the Patriots down the field. He threw a 1-yard touchdown pass to Mike Vrabel. New England made its two-point conversion. Carolina now trailed 29–22 with 2:51 left.

But the Panthers had been called the "Cardiac Cats" because they had rallied for so many heart-stopping wins during the regular season. They had come this far. Carolina was not going to fold now.

Delhomme marched the Panthers down the field. His 12-yard touchdown pass to wide receiver Ricky Proehl, followed by Kasay's extra point, tied the score at 29–29. There was only 1:08 left to play.

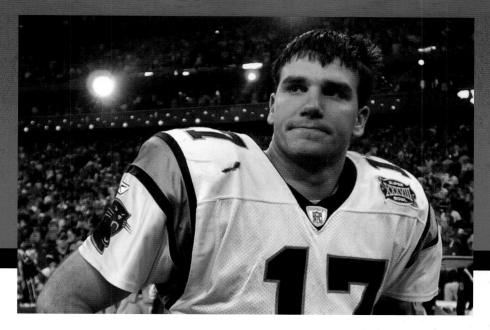

Jake Delhomme reacts after Carolina's Super Bowl loss. At the time, his 323 passing yards were his second most in an NFL game.

But that was plenty of time for Brady to advance the ball into field-goal range. He made a number of key plays down the stretch. The final one was a 17-yard pass to Deion Branch on third down to give New England a shot at a field goal.

Adam Vinatieri made the 41-yarder to give New England a 32–29 lead. The Patriots held on for the last few seconds to win a classic Super Bowl. The "Cardiac Cats" were heartbroken.

Carolina's remarkable season had not ended the way the team wanted. But the Panthers had come a long way for a team that had struggled so much just two years earlier and had only begun playing in the NFL in 1995.

CHAPTER 2

THE
QUICK RISE

Businessman and former NFL player Jerry Richardson had a dream. He wanted to bring professional football to his home state of North Carolina. For six years, Richardson worked to convince the league to grant him a franchise.

His dream became a reality on October 26, 1993. That was the date the NFL announced two new expansion teams. One was to play in Jacksonville, Florida. The other belonged to Richardson.

The entire franchise had a lot to do to get ready to play by 1995. It chose the nickname Panthers and the team colors of black, blue, and silver. The team would be referred to simply as "Carolina" to represent both North Carolina and South Carolina.

Linebacker Sam Mills was one of Carolina's early stars.

Dom Capers was selected to be Carolina's first head coach. Capers had been a successful defensive coordinator for the Pittsburgh Steelers.

Next up was the expansion draft, when Carolina selected 35 veterans who'd been made available by their former teams. Then in their first NFL Draft, the Panthers acquired 11 college players. Among them was former Penn State University star quarterback Kerry Collins, the Panthers' first draft choice.

They also stocked their roster with free agents. The Panthers picked up some of the top players in their debut season through this method, including linebackers Darion Conner, Lamar Lathon, and Sam Mills.

The Panthers played their home games in their first season at Memorial Stadium on the campus of Clemson University in South Carolina. The team's new stadium was still being built in Charlotte, North Carolina, and would not open until 1996. The Panthers struggled initially, losing their first five games. Then Carolina defeated the visiting New York Jets 26–15 on October 15 for its first regular-season win. John Kasay kicked four field goals in the victory.

The victory over the Jets was the start of a four-game winning streak. The Panthers finished their first season 7–9.

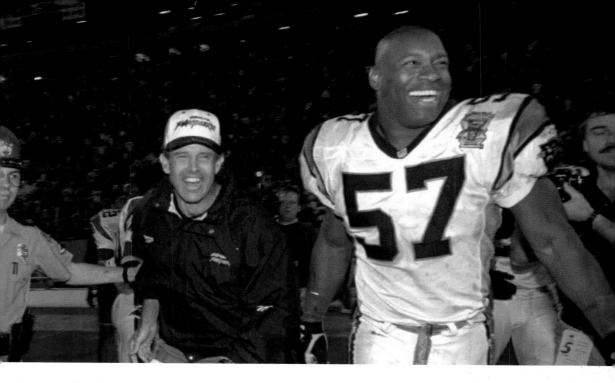

Head coach Dom Capers and linebacker Lamar Lathon are all smiles after the Panthers beat the Jets in October 1995 for their first regular-season victory.

It was the most wins ever by an expansion team. Carolina became known around the NFL as a solid defensive team.

Things went even better for the Panthers in their second season. Before it started, they signed veteran linebacker and future Hall of Famer Kevin Greene. He had been a star with the Los Angeles Rams and the Pittsburgh Steelers.

The Panthers' brand-new stadium in Charlotte was ready for the start of the 1996 season, and they made sure its inaugural season would be a memorable one. Carolina routed Atlanta 29–6 in its first regular-season home game on September 1.

SAM MILLS

The Cleveland Browns signed linebacker Sam Mills, a former star at Montclair State in New Jersey, as an undrafted free agent in 1981. But the Browns released him. They thought at 5 feet 9 inches, Mills was too short.

Mills went on to play three seasons in the United States Football League. It was a rival league to the NFL. He then signed with the New Orleans Saints and was a starter for the next nine seasons. Mills signed with the expansion Panthers in 1995. He played with them through 1997 before retiring.

After he retired, Mills stayed with the Panthers as linebackers coach. He was diagnosed with intestinal cancer during the 2003 season but continued to coach. Mills was an inspiration for Carolina during its Super Bowl run that season. Mills died on April 18, 2005, at age 45. A statue of Mills greets visitors at Carolina's stadium.

The Panthers finished the season on a seven-game winning streak. This gave Carolina a surprising 12–4 record and the NFC West title. Collins threw 14 touchdown passes in 12 starts. Tight end Wesley Walls caught 61 passes, 10 for touchdowns. Greene and Lathon combined for 28 sacks.

In the playoffs, Carolina hosted the Dallas Cowboys. The Cowboys had won three of the previous four Super Bowls. But their key players were past their primes. Collins threw for two touchdowns and Kasay made four field goals as Carolina won its first playoff game, 26–17.

✖ Adding linebacker Kevin Greene in 1996 helped the Panthers become one of the NFL's top teams in just their second season.

The Panthers went to chilly Green Bay to face the Packers and star quarterback Brett Favre in the NFC Championship Game. Carolina jumped out to an early lead behind a touchdown pass by Collins. But the Panthers' defense had no answer for the Packers' powerful offense. Green Bay rolled to a 30–13 victory. The Packers went on to win the Super Bowl.

Carolina appeared to be a team on the rise. The defense had continued to play well. It gave up the second-fewest points in the NFL. But the Panthers would discover that continued success in the NFL does not come easy.

CHAPTER 3

HITTING
ROCK BOTTOM

The good feelings from the 1996 season did not last long for the Panthers. Star linebacker Kevin Greene held out for more money. Carolina released him. He ended up with the San Francisco 49ers. Linebacker Sam Mills, at age 38, finally started to slow down and would retire at the end of the season. Linebacker Lamar Lathon did not have a strong year. As a result, the Panthers struggled in 1997. Carolina finished 7–9 and missed the playoffs.

Greene returned to the Panthers for the 1998 season. He was just as dominant as he had been in 1996. But the team quickly fell apart. The season started poorly. Quarterback Kerry Collins asked to be taken out of the lineup. Head coach Dom Capers, thinking the quarterback had quit the

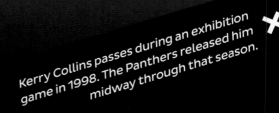

Kerry Collins passes during an exhibition game in 1998. The Panthers released him midway through that season.

✕ Quarterback Steve Beuerlein and coach George Seifert consult on the sideline during a game in 1999.

team, released Collins. That made Steve Beuerlein the starting quarterback for the rest of 1998. The Panthers fell all the way to 0–7 before they finally earned their first win of the year. Carolina won its final two games to finish 4–12.

One day after the 1998 season ended, Capers was fired. He was replaced by former San Francisco 49ers head coach George Seifert. Seifert went 98–30 with the 49ers from 1989 to 1996, and he led them to a Super Bowl championship in his first season in San Francisco. Like Capers, Seifert was known as a defense-oriented coach.

Carolina struggled at the beginning of the 1999 season. But the Panthers ended the year on a high note by winning three of their final four games. They finished 8–8. The big surprise was that Carolina won with offense. The Panthers averaged nearly 35 points in those final four games. Beuerlein set a team record with 36 touchdown passes and made the Pro Bowl. Wide receiver Muhsin Muhammad and tight end Wesley Walls also made the Pro Bowl.

But the Panthers struggled in 2000 and went 7–9. For the first time in Seifert's coaching career, one of his teams finished below .500. In the final game of the season, Carolina suffered its biggest

MUHSIN MUHAMMAD

The Panthers selected former Michigan State University wide receiver Muhsin Muhammad in the second round of the 1996 NFL Draft. He became a full-time starter with Carolina in 1998. He developed into one of the NFL's top receivers. Muhammad had back-to-back seasons with more than 1,000 receiving yards in 1999 and 2000. He set a team record with 96 receptions in 1999 and broke it the next year with 102. Muhammad led the NFL with 16 touchdown catches and 1,405 receiving yards in 2004. Then he signed with Chicago as a free agent. Muhammad played three seasons with the Bears. But he did not have the success that he enjoyed with the Panthers. He returned to Carolina for two more seasons and then retired.

RAE CARRUTH

Rae Carruth seemed to have the world at his feet. Then everything went horribly wrong. Carruth, a former University of Colorado star, had four touchdown catches as a rookie wide receiver with the Panthers in 1997. Injuries limited him the next two seasons. But his decisions off the field ended his career and the life of an innocent woman.

On November 16, 1999, a vehicle pulled up next to the car of Cherica Adams, Carruth's girlfriend. Adams, who was eight months pregnant with Carruth's child, was shot four times. She dialed 9-1-1 and said she believed Carruth was involved. Adams's baby was saved, but Adams died.

Carruth was arrested and charged with four crimes, including conspiracy to commit murder. He was convicted of three counts in 2001 and given a prison sentence of 18 to 24 years. After serving 18 years, he was released in 2018.

defeat ever. The Panthers lost 52–9 to the host Oakland Raiders on Christmas Eve.

The worst was still to come. The Panthers won their season opener in 2001. But they went on to lose their next 15 games and finished with a miserable 1–15 record. Carolina lost in every way imaginable. Chris Weinke, a 29-year-old rookie who had won the Heisman Trophy at Florida State University, was the Panthers' starting quarterback that year.

✕ Quarterback Chris Weinke tries to get rid of the ball in 2001. The Panthers finished 1–15 that season.

Seifert was fired after the season and replaced by another defensive-minded coach. John Fox had been the New York Giants' defensive coordinator. He helped New York reach Super Bowl XXXV after the 2000 season. The Panthers pinned their hopes on his ability to do the same in Carolina.

CHAPTER 4

THE RETURN TO GLORY

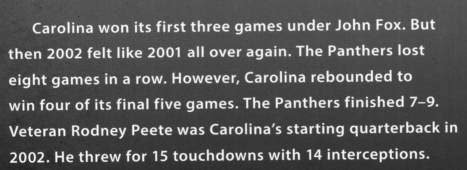

In 2002 the Panthers found themselves with a new head coach and a new division. Carolina joined the newly formed NFC South with Atlanta, New Orleans, and Tampa Bay.

Carolina won its first three games under John Fox. But then 2002 felt like 2001 all over again. The Panthers lost eight games in a row. However, Carolina rebounded to win four of its final five games. The Panthers finished 7–9. Veteran Rodney Peete was Carolina's starting quarterback in 2002. He threw for 15 touchdowns with 14 interceptions.

The Panthers' defensive improvement under Fox was immediate. They gave up the fifth-fewest points in the NFL

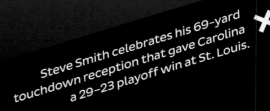

Steve Smith celebrates his 69-yard touchdown reception that gave Carolina a 29–23 playoff win at St. Louis.

JULIUS PEPPERS

One of the reasons Carolina improved on defense in 2002 was the addition of Julius Peppers. The Panthers selected the defensive end in the first round, second overall, in the 2002 NFL Draft.

Peppers was a North Carolina native and had been a star player just down the road at the University of North Carolina. He was a remarkable athlete. In addition to excelling on the gridiron, the 6-foot-6, 280-pound Peppers played for the Tar Heels' renowned basketball program.

Strength and speed were Peppers's calling cards. He had 12 sacks in 2002 and was named the NFL's Defensive Rookie of the Year. Peppers would continue to torment NFL offenses for years to come. He had 10 sacks or more in six of his first eight seasons with Carolina. Peppers was selected to five Pro Bowls with the Panthers.

Peppers left the Panthers in 2010. He then played four seasons in Chicago and three seasons in Green Bay before returning to Carolina in 2017. He played two more seasons with the Panthers before announcing his retirement in February 2019.

in 2002. In 2001 they had ranked twenty-eighth in that category. However, Carolina's offense continued to struggle in 2002.

In an attempt to improve the offense, Fox brought in two free agents before the 2003 season: running back Stephen Davis and quarterback Jake Delhomme. Davis was coming off four strong seasons in Washington. Delhomme had been stuck

DeShaun Foster breaks a tackle to score a touchdown in the Panthers' NFC title game win at Philadelphia.

on the bench with New Orleans. But Fox had liked what he had seen of Delhomme.

Both signings worked out well. Davis set a Carolina record for rushing yards in a season with 1,444. Delhomme, meanwhile, took over for Peete during the first game of the season and remained the starter.

Behind their new stars, the Panthers climbed from thirtieth to fifteenth in the NFL in points scored. Combined with its strong defense, Carolina finished the year 11–5 and in first place in the NFC South. The team peaked at the right time and made its magical run to the Super Bowl.

Panthers defensive linemen Julius Peppers, *left*, and Jordan Carstens sack Giants quarterback Eli Manning during Carolina's playoff victory at New York in January 2006.

Injuries kept the Panthers from repeating that kind of success the next season. Star wide receiver Steve Smith broke his leg in the first game. Davis suffered a knee injury shortly thereafter. Carolina got off to a 1–7 start. However, the Panthers rebounded to win six of their final eight games to go 7–9. Delhomme continued to play well.

The Panthers were healthy again in 2005. They rebounded to win the NFC South with an 11–5 record. Smith led the NFL with 103 catches, 1,563 receiving yards, and 12 touchdown receptions and won the Comeback Player of the Year Award.

Carolina reached its third NFC Championship Game in team history thanks to road victories over the New York Giants (23–0) and the Chicago Bears (29–21). Third-year running back DeShaun Foster rushed for 151 yards against the Giants. In the Bears game, Smith had 12 catches for 218 yards and two touchdowns.

But the Panthers ran out of steam in the NFC title game. Quarterback Matt Hasselbeck and running back Shaun Alexander led the Seattle Seahawks to a 34–14 victory over visiting Carolina. The Seahawks intercepted three of Delhomme's passes in the victory.

The Panthers were disappointed in the way the season had ended. Still, they had advanced as far as the NFC title game for the second time in three seasons. They figured more bright days were ahead.

STEPHEN DAVIS

South Carolina native Stephen Davis signed with the Panthers in 2003 and rushed for a career-high 1,444 yards. In the playoffs, Davis added 315 yards and a touchdown rushing despite battling injuries. Knee injuries limited Davis to 204 carries over the next two seasons. He left to play for the St. Louis Rams in 2006 but retired after that season. Davis had just one big year for the Panthers. But he was a key reason the 2003 team made it all the way to the Super Bowl.

CHAPTER 5

DOUBLE TROUBLE

The Panthers had high hopes going into the 2006 season. They had made the playoffs twice in the previous three seasons. But injuries to wide receiver Steve Smith and quarterback Jake Delhomme made 2006 a year of frustration.

The Panthers finished 8–8. It was more of the same in 2007. Delhomme was injured in the third game and missed the rest of the year. The right-hander had ligament replacement surgery in his throwing arm. Carolina went 7–9.

The Panthers looked forward to Delhomme's return in 2008. An incident during training camp threatened to distract the team, however. On August 1, Smith and teammate Ken Lucas, a cornerback, got into a fight. Smith broke Lucas's nose. Smith reportedly apologized to

Panthers running backs Jonathan Stewart and DeAngelo Williams celebrate a touchdown in 2008.

Lucas the day of the scuffle. But the team sent Smith home and eventually decided to suspend him for the first two regular-season games.

Despite missing those two games, Smith had another great season. In 14 games he caught 78 passes for 1,421 yards and scored six touchdowns. He was selected to the Pro Bowl.

But the biggest story of the 2008 season for the Panthers was the emergence of two young running backs who helped the team get back to the playoffs. Many wondered whether third-year back DeAngelo Williams or rookie Jonathan Stewart would be the team's main runner. Coach John Fox ended up featuring both backs. Williams was officially the starter. But Stewart received more playing time than a typical backup. The youngsters became known as "Double Trouble."

In Week 5, Williams ran for three touchdowns as Carolina defeated the visiting Kansas City Chiefs 34–0 to improve to 4–1. It was the first of five games that year in which Williams would score multiple touchdowns. He finished the season with 1,515 rushing yards, breaking Stephen Davis's team record. Williams also scored 20 touchdowns (18 rushing, two receiving) to top Muhsin Muhammad's Panthers record of 16, set in 2004.

Carolina's DeAngelo Williams breaks away for a big gain. Williams's 1,515 rushing yards in 2008 were more than double what he had the previous season.

Meanwhile, Stewart finished the season with 836 rushing yards and 10 touchdowns. The strong ground game led the Panthers to a 12–4 record and an NFC South title.

Carolina hosted the Arizona Cardinals in the divisional round of the playoffs. Stewart opened the scoring with a 9-yard touchdown run. But the Cardinals scored the next 33 points to win 33–13. The Panthers were disappointed that they had not played better, especially considering that the game was at home. Delhomme threw five interceptions. Carolina committed six turnovers in all.

STEVE SMITH

The Panthers originally used Steve Smith primarily as a kick returner. The former University of Utah standout scored three touchdowns on returns in his rookie season in 2001. By 2003, the speedy Smith had developed into an excellent wide receiver. He had 88 catches for 1,110 yards and seven touchdowns and helped the Panthers reach their first Super Bowl. Smith was the Panthers' top receiving threat for the 13 seasons he played in Carolina. He set the team record for most career catches (836), receiving yards (12,197), and touchdown catches (67).

Double Trouble had another big season in 2009. Stewart set a team single-game record with 206 rushing yards in a 41–9 win over the New York Giants. He finished the season with 1,133 rushing yards and 11 total touchdowns. Williams, meanwhile, ran for 1,117 yards and seven touchdowns despite battling injuries and missing three games. It was just the sixth time in NFL history that two teammates had rushed for 1,000 yards in the same season. They were the first to both top 1,100 yards. The Panthers finished 8–8 and missed the playoffs. But the play of the Double Trouble tandem continued to give Panthers fans hope for the future.

Delhomme's performance in 2009 was disappointing. He threw just eight touchdown passes and 18 interceptions in 11 games. By December backup Matt Moore had taken over as

Quarterback Jake Delhomme is harassed by Cardinals defensive end Calais Campbell in Carolina's playoff loss to Arizona in January 2009.

the starting quarterback. He played well, and the Panthers won their final three games.

On March 5, 2010, the Panthers made the difficult decision to release Delhomme. The same day, Julius Peppers, the team's dynamic defensive end, signed a free-agent contract with the Chicago Bears. It was the end of an era for the Panthers. But a new one was just about to begin.

CHAPTER 6

SUPERCAM'S
SUPER BOWL

History practically repeated itself for the Panthers in 2010. It was not as bad as the season they had in 2001, but it was close. Everything went wrong as Carolina went 2–14. Just like after the 2001 season, the head coach was fired.

Panthers fans hoped another aspect of that history also would be part of the new future. They hoped the new guy would take the Panthers to the Super Bowl.

The new guy was Ron Rivera. Like John Fox in 2002, he was a first-time head coach. But Rivera knew what it took to make it to the big game. He had played in Super Bowl XX as a linebacker with the 1985 Chicago Bears.

Carolina also needed a new quarterback. The Panthers started four different players at the position in 2010, and

Cam Newton poses with NFL Commissioner Roger Goodell at the 2011 NFL Draft.

When Ron Rivera was hired as Panthers head coach, he was known as a defensive genius. He had led the San Diego Chargers top-ranked defense in 2010 as defensive coordinator. And he played on one of the best defenses ever with the 1985 Chicago Bears. But he also built Carolina into one of the league's best offenses. Rivera earned the nickname "Riverboat Ron" for sometimes gambling and taking risks with his play calling.

none of them were effective. Because the team had the worst record in the NFL, the Panthers got to pick first in the draft.

The Panthers selected quarterback Cam Newton from Auburn University. Newton was a Heisman Trophy winner. He also was an amazing athlete. Newton could pass and was a strong runner.

The Panthers improved by four wins in 2011. And Newton was named the NFL Offensive Rookie of the Year. He started all 16 games, throwing for 4,051 yards and 21 touchdowns. He also carried the ball 126 times for 706 yards and 14 touchdowns. With Newton, DeAngelo Williams (836 yards), and Jonathan Stewart (761 yards), the Panthers had a dominant rushing attack.

The Carolina defense got a huge boost in 2012 when the Panthers used their first-round pick to draft Boston College linebacker Luke Kuechly. With a league-leading 165 tackles in 2012, Kuechly was named the NFL Defensive Rookie of the Year.

✖ Linebacker Luke Kuechly wraps up Atlanta's Jacquizz Rodgers in 2012.

With young stars on both sides of the ball, the Panthers improved to 12–4 and won the NFC South in 2013. Kuechly was named the NFL Defensive Player of the Year while Rivera won NFL Coach of the Year honors. But Carolina suffered a disappointing 23–10 playoff loss to the San Francisco 49ers.

Despite slipping to a 7–8–1 record in 2014, the Panthers still managed to repeat as NFC South champions. And they even won a playoff game for the first time since January 2006.

Winning a playoff game was a big step. But the Panthers knew they could do better. Newton had the worst year of his career. He set career lows in passing and rushing yards. Carolina needed him to do better to get them to the next level.

KEEP POUNDING

More than a decade after his death, linebacker Sam Mills was still a major figure in Panthers history. His motivational motto was "Keep Pounding." It meant to keep fighting no matter what the challenge was. It applied to both his cancer fight and football. Mills's words were added to a drum that a special guest beats four times before every Panthers home game. The phrase appears all around Bank of America Stadium as well.

That's exactly what Newton did. He threw 35 touchdown passes and only 10 interceptions. He ran for 10 more touchdowns. Newton was named the NFL Offensive Player of the Year and Most Valuable Player. His talent earned him the nickname "SuperCam."

Newton was now the second leading rusher on the team behind Stewart. Double Trouble had split the previous year when Williams left for Pittsburgh. Newton also had a star receiver in tight end Greg Olsen, who caught 77 passes for 1,104 yards. Led by Kuechly, the Panthers had a top-10 defense, too.

Carolina went 15–1, the best record in team history. Then it was time to avenge some playoff defeats. After winning a close game over the Seattle Seahawks in the divisional round, the Panthers hammered the Arizona Cardinals in the NFC Championship Game. Newton threw for two touchdowns and ran for two more as the Panthers won 49–15.

The Broncos applied heavy pressure on Newton (1) throughout the Super Bowl.

They were going back to the Super Bowl. Like the first time around, their opponent was a legendary quarterback. This time it was Peyton Manning and the Denver Broncos.

The Broncos got the ball first. Manning led them down the field, but they had to settle for a field goal. After the teams traded punts, disaster struck. From his own 15-yard line, Newton dropped back to pass. Broncos linebacker Von Miller sacked him and forced a fumble. Denver recovered it in the end zone for a touchdown.

The Panthers' offense bounced back in the second quarter with a 1-yard touchdown by Stewart. But the offense was shut out the rest of the way as Carolina trailed 13–7 at halftime.

That was as close as they got. In the second half, the Broncos' defense was too tough. The Panthers' defense played great, too, holding Manning to just 141 passing yards. But it wasn't enough. The Broncos pulled away from Carolina and won 24–10.

The Panthers failed to build on their Super Bowl breakthrough. They started 2016 1–5 and finished 6–10. Injuries and the loss of key players took a toll.

ONE CAROLINA

The Panthers are unusual among American sports teams. They are referred to by a region, not a city or state. That is because the Panthers represent both North Carolina and South Carolina. When the Panthers made their run to Super Bowl 50, the hashtag #OneCarolina was developed. It symbolized that when it comes to rooting for the Panthers, both Carolinas were in it together.

A familiar face boosted the team in 2017. Defensive end Julius Peppers returned after seven years. Though he was 37, he still could play at a high level. On offense, the team had a dynamic new weapon in running back Christian McCaffrey, who caught 80 passes out of the backfield and posted nearly 1,100 total yards. The Panthers made it back to the playoffs as a wild card but lost to the New Orleans Saints.

Panthers running back Christian McCaffrey had a breakout season in 2018.

After 10 seasons in Carolina, Stewart left as a free agent in 2018. His 7,318 rushing yards were the most in team history. But McCaffrey filled the role spectacularly. He led the team in both rushing and receiving yards and set an NFL single-season record for running backs with 106 receptions. Still, the Panthers finished 7–9 and out of the playoffs.

Getting to the Super Bowl is never easy. But the Panthers still had the core of talent to make a run. After all, they bounced back from 1–15 and 2–14 seasons. They've shown they can never be counted out.

TIMELINE

On October 26, the NFL awards Jerry Richardson an expansion franchise. The team will be called the Carolina Panthers.

The Panthers hire former Pittsburgh Steelers defensive coordinator Dom Capers as their first head coach on January 23.

In their first regular-season game, the Panthers lose 23–20 in overtime to the host Atlanta Falcons on September 3.

On October 15, Carolina beats the New York Jets 26–15 to get its first regular-season win.

The Panthers open their brand-new stadium for an exhibition game against the Chicago Bears on August 3.

1993

1995

1995

1995

1996

On January 5, host Carolina earns its first playoff win on its first try with a 26–17 victory over the Dallas Cowboys.

Former San Francisco 49ers coach George Seifert is hired to replace Capers as the Panthers' second head coach on January 4.

Former New York Giants defensive coordinator John Fox becomes the Panthers' third head coach on January 25.

With the second overall pick in the NFL Draft, the Panthers select Julius Peppers from the University of North Carolina.

The Panthers capture their first NFC title with a 14–3 road win over the Philadelphia Eagles on January 18.

1997

1999

2002

2002

2004

On February 1, Carolina loses its first Super Bowl 32–29 when Patriots kicker Adam Vinatieri makes a 41-yard field goal with four seconds left.

Former Panthers linebacker Sam Mills dies on April 18 at the age of 45 after a fight with intestinal cancer. The team retires his No. 51 later that season.

The Panthers tie an NFL record with their fourth road playoff victory in a row, a 29–21 win over the Chicago Bears on January 15.

On December 14, Carolina beats the Denver Broncos 30–10 to finish the regular season 8–0 at home for the second time in team history.

Jonathan Stewart and DeAngelo Williams become the first teammates to each rush for 1,100 yards in the same season.

2004

2005

2006

2008

2009

Ron Rivera takes over as head coach, and the team selects quarterback Cam Newton with the first overall pick in the NFL Draft.

The Panthers draft linebacker Luke Kuechly from Boston College ninth overall. Kuechly wins the Defensive Rookie of the Year Award.

Kuechly is named the NFL Defensive Player of the Year and Rivera the NFL Coach of the Year as the Panthers go 12–4 and win the NFC South.

Newton wins the NFL MVP Award after leading the Panthers to a 15–1 record. They make it to the Super Bowl but lose to the Denver Broncos.

Christian McCaffrey catches 106 passes, the most ever in one season by an NFL running back, as the Panthers go 7–9.

2011

2012

2013

2015

2018

QUICK STATS

FRANCHISE HISTORY

1995–

SUPER BOWLS

2003 (XXXVIII), 2015 (50)

DIVISION CHAMPIONSHIPS

1996, 2003, 2008, 2013, 2014, 2015

PLAYOFF APPEARANCES

1996, 2003, 2005, 2008, 2013, 2014, 2015, 2017

NFC CHAMPIONSHIP GAMES

1996, 2003, 2005, 2015

KEY COACHES

Dom Capers (1995–98): 30–34, 1–1 (playoffs)
John Fox (2002–10): 73–71, 5–3 (playoffs)
Ron Rivera (2011–): 71–56–1, 3–4 (playoffs)

KEY PLAYERS
(position, seasons with team)

Michael Bates (KR/DB, 1996–2000)
Kerry Collins (QB, 1995–98)
Thomas Davis (LB, 2005–18)
Jake Delhomme (QB, 2003–09)
Kevin Greene (LB, 1996, 1998–99)
John Kasay (K, 1995–2010)
Luke Kuechly (LB, 2012–)
Sam Mills (LB, 1995–97)
Mike Minter (S, 1997–2006)
Muhsin Muhammad
    (WR, 1996–2004, 2008–09)
Cam Newton (QB, 2011–)
Greg Olsen (TE, 2011–)
Julius Peppers (DE, 2002–09, 2017–18)
Mike Rucker (DE, 1999–2007)
Steve Smith (WR, 2001–13)
Jonathan Stewart (RB, 2008–17)
Wesley Walls (TE, 1996–2002)
DeAngelo Williams (RB, 2006–14)

HOME FIELDS

Bank of America Stadium (1996–)
    Also known as Ericsson Stadium
Clemson Memorial Stadium (1995)

* All statistics through 2018 season

QUOTES AND ANECDOTES

"Kicking a football is very simple. I did it in my backyard at the age of four. But put 11 guys on the other side, fill the stadium with 70,000 screaming fans, battle it out for three hours, and have the outcome of the game determined by that final kick—it's no longer quite so simple."

—Carolina place kicker John Kasay

John Kasay was a fourth-round pick of the Seattle Seahawks in 1991. The left-footed kicker played at the University of Georgia. He spent four seasons with Seattle before joining Carolina in time for its first season in 1995. Kasay immediately established his worth with Carolina by making three game-winning kicks in 1995. In 1996 Kasay led the NFL with 145 points and made 37 field goals to set a new league record, which has since been broken. On December 6, 2009, Kasay made the 400th field goal of his career. He became only the seventh player in NFL history to accomplish the feat. He played with the Panthers through 2010.

"Sam was one of the finest people you will ever meet. You would never know that he was a player who made Pro Bowls and had all this attention because he treated everybody the same no matter who they were. He never had a bad thing to say about anybody and had a great ability to laugh at himself. He was the type of guy you want your kids to grow up to be."

—Carolina general manager Marty Hurney, on former Panthers linebacker Sam Mills.

Visitors to Bank of America Stadium are greeted by a snarling panther statue at each gate. Each of the six panthers is 8 feet (2.4 m) tall and weighs 2,000 pounds (907 kg). In 2016 the team added a 13-foot (4 m) statue of owner Jerry Richardson flanked by two more snarling panthers.

GLOSSARY

cardiac
Relating to the heart; often used in reference to a heart attack.

conspiracy
A secret plan by a group to do something unlawful or harmful.

coordinator
An assistant coach who is in charge of the offense or defense.

draft
A system that allows teams to acquire new players coming into a league.

dynamic
Energetic and forceful.

expansion
The addition of new teams to increase the size of a league.

franchise
A sports organization, including the top-level team and all minor league affiliates.

free agent
A player whose rights are not owned by any team.

Heisman Trophy
The award given yearly to the best player in college football.

Pro Bowl
The NFL's all-star game, in which the best players in the league compete.

two-point conversion
An option for teams that have scored a touchdown to try a running or passing play from the 2-yard line for two points, instead of kicking for one point.

MORE INFORMATION

BOOKS

DiPrimio, Pete. *Cam Newton*. Kennett Square, PA: Purple Toad Publishing, 2017.

Kortemeier, Todd. *Carolina Panthers*. Minneapolis, MN: Abdo Publishing, 2017.

Lajiness, Katie. *Carolina Panthers*. Minneapolis, MN: Big Buddy Books, 2017.

ONLINE RESOURCES

Booklinks
NONFICTION NETWORK
FREE! ONLINE NONFICTION RESOURCES

To learn more about the Carolina Panthers, visit **abdobooklinks.com** or scan this QR code. These links are routinely monitored and updated to provide the most current information available.

PLACE TO VISIT

Bank of America Stadium
800 South Mint St.
Charlotte, NC 28202
704–358–7000
panthers.com/stadium

The home of the Carolina Panthers is a 75,525-seat open-air stadium. Look for statues honoring former general manager and president Mike McCormack and linebacker Sam Mills.

INDEX

ABOUT THE AUTHOR

Todd Ryan is a library assistant from the Upper Peninsula of Michigan. He lives near Houghton with his two cats, Izzo and Mooch.